MY BOAT DETAILS

NAME:	LENGTH:
MODEL:	DRAFT:
SERIAL NO:	BEAM:

ENGINE DETAILS

MODEL:	SERIAL NO:
HP/KWH:	CAPACITY:
OIL TYPE:	FILTER LOCATION:
MANUFACTURER:	YEAR MANUFACTURED:

FUEL DETAILS

TYPE:	TANK SIZE:
TANK LOCATION:	FILL LOCATION:

BATTERY DETAILS

MODEL:	SERIAL NO:
SIZE:	EFFICIENCY:

HEAD DETAILS

MODEL:	TYPE:
CAPACITY:	MANUFACTURER:

TRANSMISSION DETAILS

MODEL:	OIL CAPACITY:
OIL TYPE:	MANUFACTURER:

ROUTINE MAINTENANCE TASKS

DATE	MAINTENANCE TASKS	NOTES

ROUTINE MAINTENANCE TASKS

DATE	MAINTENANCE TASKS	NOTES

ROUTINE MAINTENANCE TASKS

DATE	MAINTENANCE TASKS	NOTES

ROUTINE MAINTENANCE TASKS

DATE	MAINTENANCE TASKS	NOTES

WORK LOG

DATE	ENGINE HRS	REPAIR	MAINTENANCE	DONE BY

| DATE | ENGINE HRS | REPAIR | MAINTENANCE | DONE BY |

WORK LOG

DATE	ENGINE HRS	REPAIR	MAINTENANCE	DONE BY
DATE	ENGINE HRS	REPAIR	MAINTENANCE	DONE BY

WORK LOG

DATE	ENGINE HRS	REPAIR	MAINTENANCE	DONE BY
DATE	ENGINE HRS	REPAIR	MAINTENANCE	DONE BY

WORK LOG

DATE	ENGINE HRS	REPAIR	MAINTENANCE	DONE BY
DATE	ENGINE HRS	REPAIR	MAINTENANCE	DONE BY

WORK LOG

DATE	ENGINE HRS	REPAIR	MAINTENANCE	DONE BY
DATE	ENGINE HRS	REPAIR	MAINTENANCE	DONE BY

WORK LOG

DATE	ENGINE HRS	REPAIR	MAINTENANCE	DONE BY
DATE	ENGINE HRS	REPAIR	MAINTENANCE	DONE BY

WORK LOG

DATE	ENGINE HRS	REPAIR	MAINTENANCE	DONE BY

| DATE | ENGINE HRS | REPAIR | MAINTENANCE | DONE BY |

WORK LOG

DATE	ENGINE HRS	REPAIR	MAINTENANCE	DONE BY

DATE	ENGINE HRS	REPAIR	MAINTENANCE	DONE BY

WORK LOG

DATE	ENGINE HRS	REPAIR	MAINTENANCE	DONE BY
DATE	ENGINE HRS	REPAIR	MAINTENANCE	DONE BY

WORK LOG

DATE	ENGINE HRS	REPAIR	MAINTENANCE	DONE BY
DATE	ENGINE HRS	REPAIR	MAINTENANCE	DONE BY

WORK LOG

DATE	ENGINE HRS	REPAIR	MAINTENANCE	DONE BY

| DATE | ENGINE HRS | REPAIR | MAINTENANCE | DONE BY |

WORK LOG

DATE	ENGINE HRS	REPAIR	MAINTENANCE	DONE BY
DATE	ENGINE HRS	REPAIR	MAINTENANCE	DONE BY

WORK LOG

DATE	ENGINE HRS	REPAIR	MAINTENANCE	DONE BY
DATE	ENGINE HRS	REPAIR	MAINTENANCE	DONE BY

WORK LOG

DATE	ENGINE HRS	REPAIR	MAINTENANCE	DONE BY
DATE	ENGINE HRS	REPAIR	MAINTENANCE	DONE BY

WORK LOG

DATE	ENGINE HRS	REPAIR	MAINTENANCE	DONE BY

WORK LOG

DATE	ENGINE HRS	REPAIR	MAINTENANCE	DONE BY
DATE	ENGINE HRS	REPAIR	MAINTENANCE	DONE BY

WORK LOG

DATE	ENGINE HRS	REPAIR	MAINTENANCE	DONE BY
DATE	ENGINE HRS	REPAIR	MAINTENANCE	DONE BY

WORK LOG

DATE	ENGINE HRS	REPAIR	MAINTENANCE	DONE BY
DATE	ENGINE HRS	REPAIR	MAINTENANCE	DONE BY

WORK LOG

DATE	ENGINE HRS	REPAIR	MAINTENANCE	DONE BY

| DATE | ENGINE HRS | REPAIR | MAINTENANCE | DONE BY |

WORK LOG

DATE	ENGINE HRS	REPAIR	MAINTENANCE	DONE BY
DATE	ENGINE HRS	REPAIR	MAINTENANCE	DONE BY

WORK LOG

DATE	ENGINE HRS	REPAIR	MAINTENANCE	DONE BY
DATE	ENGINE HRS	REPAIR	MAINTENANCE	DONE BY

WORK LOG

DATE	ENGINE HRS	REPAIR	MAINTENANCE	DONE BY
DATE	ENGINE HRS	REPAIR	MAINTENANCE	DONE BY

WORK LOG

DATE	ENGINE HRS	REPAIR	MAINTENANCE	DONE BY

WORK LOG

DATE	ENGINE HRS	REPAIR	MAINTENANCE	DONE BY
DATE	ENGINE HRS	REPAIR	MAINTENANCE	DONE BY

WORK LOG

DATE	ENGINE HRS	REPAIR	MAINTENANCE	DONE BY

DATE	ENGINE HRS	REPAIR	MAINTENANCE	DONE BY

WORK LOG

DATE	ENGINE HRS	REPAIR	MAINTENANCE	DONE BY
DATE	ENGINE HRS	REPAIR	MAINTENANCE	DONE BY

WORK LOG

DATE	ENGINE HRS	REPAIR	MAINTENANCE	DONE BY

WORK LOG

DATE	ENGINE HRS	REPAIR	MAINTENANCE	DONE BY
DATE	ENGINE HRS	REPAIR	MAINTENANCE	DONE BY

WORK LOG

DATE	ENGINE HRS	REPAIR	MAINTENANCE	DONE BY
DATE	ENGINE HRS	REPAIR	MAINTENANCE	DONE BY

WORK LOG

DATE	ENGINE HRS	REPAIR	MAINTENANCE	DONE BY

WORK LOG

DATE	ENGINE HRS	REPAIR	MAINTENANCE	DONE BY
DATE	ENGINE HRS	REPAIR	MAINTENANCE	DONE BY

WORK LOG

DATE	ENGINE HRS	REPAIR	MAINTENANCE	DONE BY
DATE	ENGINE HRS	REPAIR	MAINTENANCE	DONE BY

WORK LOG

DATE	ENGINE HRS	REPAIR	MAINTENANCE	DONE BY
DATE	ENGINE HRS	REPAIR	MAINTENANCE	DONE BY

WORK LOG

DATE	ENGINE HRS		REPAIR	MAINTENANCE	DONE BY
DATE	ENGINE HRS		REPAIR	MAINTENANCE	DONE BY

WORK LOG

DATE	ENGINE HRS	REPAIR	MAINTENANCE	DONE BY

WORK LOG

DATE	ENGINE HRS	REPAIR	MAINTENANCE	DONE BY
DATE	ENGINE HRS	REPAIR	MAINTENANCE	DONE BY

WORK LOG

DATE	ENGINE HRS	REPAIR	MAINTENANCE	DONE BY

WORK LOG

DATE	ENGINE HRS	REPAIR	MAINTENANCE	DONE BY
DATE	ENGINE HRS	REPAIR	MAINTENANCE	DONE BY

WORK LOG

DATE	ENGINE HRS	REPAIR	MAINTENANCE	DONE BY

WORK LOG

DATE	ENGINE HRS	REPAIR	MAINTENANCE	DONE BY
DATE	ENGINE HRS	REPAIR	MAINTENANCE	DONE BY

WORK LOG

DATE	ENGINE HRS	REPAIR	MAINTENANCE	DONE BY

WORK LOG

DATE	ENGINE HRS	REPAIR	MAINTENANCE	DONE BY

| DATE | ENGINE HRS | REPAIR | MAINTENANCE | DONE BY |

WORK LOG

DATE	ENGINE HRS	REPAIR	MAINTENANCE	DONE BY

WORK LOG

DATE	ENGINE HRS	REPAIR	MAINTENANCE	DONE BY
DATE	ENGINE HRS	REPAIR	MAINTENANCE	DONE BY

WORK LOG

DATE	ENGINE HRS	REPAIR	MAINTENANCE	DONE BY

DATE	ENGINE HRS	REPAIR	MAINTENANCE	DONE BY

WORK LOG

DATE	ENGINE HRS	REPAIR	MAINTENANCE	DONE BY

DATE	ENGINE HRS	REPAIR	MAINTENANCE	DONE BY

WORK LOG

DATE	ENGINE HRS	REPAIR	MAINTENANCE	DONE BY

DATE	ENGINE HRS	REPAIR	MAINTENANCE	DONE BY

WORK LOG

DATE	ENGINE HRS	REPAIR	MAINTENANCE	DONE BY
DATE	ENGINE HRS	REPAIR	MAINTENANCE	DONE BY

WORK LOG

DATE	ENGINE HRS	REPAIR	MAINTENANCE	DONE BY

DATE	ENGINE HRS	REPAIR	MAINTENANCE	DONE BY

WORK LOG

DATE	ENGINE HRS	REPAIR	MAINTENANCE	DONE BY

WORK LOG

DATE	ENGINE HRS	REPAIR	MAINTENANCE	DONE BY

| DATE | ENGINE HRS | REPAIR | MAINTENANCE | DONE BY |

WORK LOG

DATE	ENGINE HRS	REPAIR	MAINTENANCE	DONE BY

WORK LOG

DATE	ENGINE HRS	REPAIR	MAINTENANCE	DONE BY
DATE	ENGINE HRS	REPAIR	MAINTENANCE	DONE BY

WORK LOG

DATE	ENGINE HRS	REPAIR	MAINTENANCE	DONE BY
DATE	ENGINE HRS	REPAIR	MAINTENANCE	DONE BY

WORK LOG

DATE	ENGINE HRS	REPAIR	MAINTENANCE	DONE BY
DATE	ENGINE HRS	REPAIR	MAINTENANCE	DONE BY

WORK LOG

DATE	ENGINE HRS	REPAIR	MAINTENANCE	DONE BY
DATE	ENGINE HRS	REPAIR	MAINTENANCE	DONE BY

WORK LOG

DATE	ENGINE HRS	REPAIR	MAINTENANCE	DONE BY
DATE	ENGINE HRS	REPAIR	MAINTENANCE	DONE BY

WORK LOG

DATE	ENGINE HRS	REPAIR	MAINTENANCE	DONE BY

WORK LOG

DATE	ENGINE HRS	REPAIR	MAINTENANCE	DONE BY
DATE	ENGINE HRS	REPAIR	MAINTENANCE	DONE BY

WORK LOG

DATE	ENGINE HRS	REPAIR	MAINTENANCE	DONE BY
DATE	ENGINE HRS	REPAIR	MAINTENANCE	DONE BY

WORK LOG

DATE	ENGINE HRS	REPAIR	MAINTENANCE	DONE BY
DATE	ENGINE HRS	REPAIR	MAINTENANCE	DONE BY

WORK LOG

DATE	ENGINE HRS	REPAIR	MAINTENANCE	DONE BY

DATE	ENGINE HRS	REPAIR	MAINTENANCE	DONE BY

WORK LOG

DATE	ENGINE HRS	REPAIR	MAINTENANCE	DONE BY
DATE	ENGINE HRS	REPAIR	MAINTENANCE	DONE BY

WORK LOG

DATE	ENGINE HRS	REPAIR	MAINTENANCE	DONE BY
DATE	ENGINE HRS	REPAIR	MAINTENANCE	DONE BY

WORK LOG

DATE	ENGINE HRS	REPAIR	MAINTENANCE	DONE BY

WORK LOG

DATE	ENGINE HRS	REPAIR	MAINTENANCE	DONE BY

WORK LOG

DATE	ENGINE HRS	REPAIR	MAINTENANCE	DONE BY

DATE	ENGINE HRS	REPAIR	MAINTENANCE	DONE BY

WORK LOG

DATE	ENGINE HRS	REPAIR	MAINTENANCE	DONE BY

| DATE | ENGINE HRS | REPAIR | MAINTENANCE | DONE BY |

WORK LOG

DATE	ENGINE HRS	REPAIR	MAINTENANCE	DONE BY
DATE	ENGINE HRS	REPAIR	MAINTENANCE	DONE BY

WORK LOG

DATE	ENGINE HRS	REPAIR	MAINTENANCE	DONE BY

WORK LOG

DATE	ENGINE HRS	REPAIR	MAINTENANCE	DONE BY
DATE	ENGINE HRS	REPAIR	MAINTENANCE	DONE BY

WORK LOG

DATE	ENGINE HRS	REPAIR	MAINTENANCE	DONE BY
DATE	ENGINE HRS	REPAIR	MAINTENANCE	DONE BY

WORK LOG

DATE	ENGINE HRS	REPAIR	MAINTENANCE	DONE BY

| DATE | ENGINE HRS | REPAIR | MAINTENANCE | DONE BY |

WORK LOG

DATE	ENGINE HRS	REPAIR	MAINTENANCE	DONE BY

DATE	ENGINE HRS	REPAIR	MAINTENANCE	DONE BY

WORK LOG

DATE	ENGINE HRS	REPAIR	MAINTENANCE	DONE BY
DATE	ENGINE HRS	REPAIR	MAINTENANCE	DONE BY

WORK LOG

DATE	ENGINE HRS	REPAIR	MAINTENANCE	DONE BY
DATE	ENGINE HRS	REPAIR	MAINTENANCE	DONE BY

WORK LOG

DATE	ENGINE HRS	REPAIR	MAINTENANCE	DONE BY

DATE	ENGINE HRS	REPAIR	MAINTENANCE	DONE BY

WORK LOG

DATE	ENGINE HRS	REPAIR	MAINTENANCE	DONE BY
DATE	ENGINE HRS	REPAIR	MAINTENANCE	DONE BY

WORK LOG

DATE	ENGINE HRS	REPAIR	MAINTENANCE	DONE BY

WORK LOG

DATE	ENGINE HRS	REPAIR	MAINTENANCE	DONE BY
DATE	ENGINE HRS	REPAIR	MAINTENANCE	DONE BY

FUEL LOG

DATE	MILEAGE	FUEL TYPE	TOPPED UP (GL)	DONE BY

DATE	MILEAGE	FUEL TYPE	TOPPED UP (GL)	DONE BY

FUEL LOG

DATE	MILEAGE	FUEL TYPE	TOPPED UP (GL)	DONE BY

FUEL LOG

DATE	MILEAGE	FUEL TYPE	TOPPED UP (GL)	DONE BY

FUEL LOG

DATE	MILEAGE	FUEL TYPE	TOPPED UP (GL)	DONE BY

| DATE | MILEAGE | FUEL TYPE | TOPPED UP (GL) | DONE BY |

FUEL LOG

DATE	MILEAGE	FUEL TYPE	TOPPED UP (GL)	DONE BY

DATE	MILEAGE	FUEL TYPE	TOPPED UP (GL)	DONE BY

FUEL LOG

DATE	MILEAGE	FUEL TYPE	TOPPED UP (GL)	DONE BY
DATE	MILEAGE	FUEL TYPE	TOPPED UP (GL)	DONE BY

SPARE PARTS LIST

ITEM	DESCRIPTION	# OF PARTS	PART #	BUY FROM

SPARE PARTS LIST

ITEM	DESCRIPTION	# OF PARTS	PART #	BUY FROM
ITEM	DESCRIPTION	# OF PARTS	PART #	BUY FROM

SPARE PARTS LIST

ITEM	DESCRIPTION	# OF PARTS	PART #	BUY FROM
ITEM	DESCRIPTION	# OF PARTS	PART #	BUY FROM

SPARE PARTS LIST

ITEM	DESCRIPTION	# OF PARTS	PART #	BUY FROM
ITEM	DESCRIPTION	# OF PARTS	PART #	BUY FROM

SPARE PARTS LIST

ITEM	DESCRIPTION	# OF PARTS	PART #	BUY FROM

SPARE PARTS LIST

ITEM		DESCRIPTION	# OF PARTS	PART #	BUY FROM

SUPPLIERS' CONTACTS

Name	
Address	
Contact Number	
Email	
Selling which Spare Parts	

Name	
Address	
Contact Number	
Email	
Selling which Spare Parts	

Name	
Address	
Contact Number	
Email	
Selling which Spare Parts	

Name	
Address	
Contact Number	
Email	
Selling which Spare Parts	

SUPPLIERS' CONTACTS

Name	
Address	
Contact Number	
Email	
Selling which Spare Parts	

Name	
Address	
Contact Number	
Email	
Selling which Spare Parts	

Name	
Address	
Contact Number	
Email	
Selling which Spare Parts	

Name	
Address	
Contact Number	
Email	
Selling which Spare Parts	

SUPPLIERS' CONTACTS

Name	
Address	
Contact Number	
Email	
Selling which Spare Parts	

Name	
Address	
Contact Number	
Email	
Selling which Spare Parts	

Name	
Address	
Contact Number	
Email	
Selling which Spare Parts	

Name	
Address	
Contact Number	
Email	
Selling which Spare Parts	

SUPPLIERS' CONTACTS

Name	
Address	
Contact Number	
Email	
Selling which Spare Parts	

Name	
Address	
Contact Number	
Email	
Selling which Spare Parts	

Name	
Address	
Contact Number	
Email	
Selling which Spare Parts	

Name	
Address	
Contact Number	
Email	
Selling which Spare Parts	

SUPPLIERS' CONTACTS

Name	
Address	
Contact Number	
Email	
Selling which Spare Parts	

Name	
Address	
Contact Number	
Email	
Selling which Spare Parts	

Name	
Address	
Contact Number	
Email	
Selling which Spare Parts	

Name	
Address	
Contact Number	
Email	
Selling which Spare Parts	

SUPPLIERS' CONTACTS

Name	
Address	
Contact Number	
Email	
Selling which Spare Parts	

Name	
Address	
Contact Number	
Email	
Selling which Spare Parts	

Name	
Address	
Contact Number	
Email	
Selling which Spare Parts	

Name	
Address	
Contact Number	
Email	
Selling which Spare Parts	

MAINTENANCE/REPAIR SHOP'CONTACTS

Name	
Address	
Contact Number	
Email	
Notes	

Name	
Address	
Contact Number	
Email	
Notes	

Name	
Address	
Contact Number	
Email	
Notes	

Name	
Address	
Contact Number	
Email	
Notes	

MAINTENANCE/REPAIR SHOP'CONTACTS

Name	
Address	
Contact Number	
Email	
Notes	

Name	
Address	
Contact Number	
Email	
Notes	

Name	
Address	
Contact Number	
Email	
Notes	

Name	
Address	
Contact Number	
Email	
Notes	

MAINTENANCE/REPAIR SHOP CONTACTS

Name	
Address	
Contact Number	
Email	
Notes	

Name	
Address	
Contact Number	
Email	
Notes	

Name	
Address	
Contact Number	
Email	
Notes	

Name	
Address	
Contact Number	
Email	
Notes	

MAINTENANCE/REPAIR SHOP'CONTACTS

Name	
Address	
Contact Number	
Email	
Notes	

Name	
Address	
Contact Number	
Email	
Notes	

Name	
Address	
Contact Number	
Email	
Notes	

Name	
Address	
Contact Number	
Email	
Notes	

Specially Designed By:

Zen BOAT Crafts

Made in the USA
Las Vegas, NV
13 November 2023